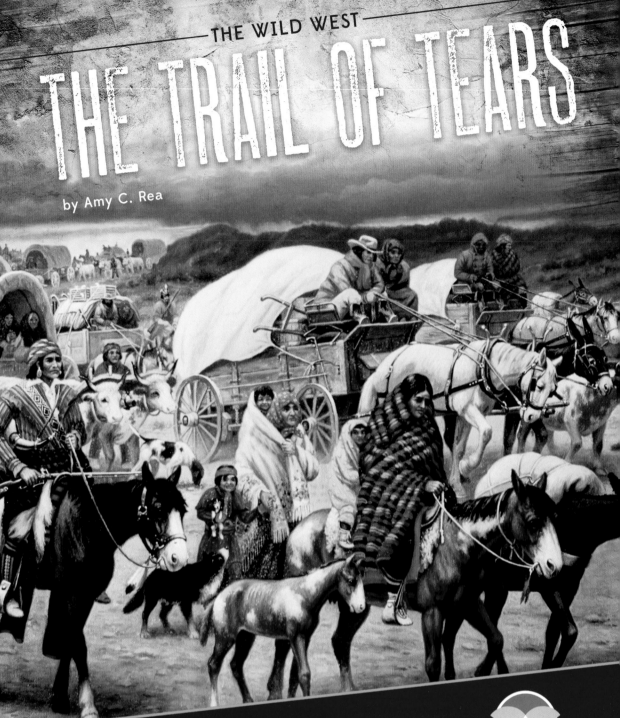

THE WILD WEST

# THE TRAIL OF TEARS

by Amy C. Rea

**Content Consultant**
Dr. James A. Bryant
Associate Professor
Appalachian State University

**Core Library**

An Imprint of Abdo Publishing
abdopublishing.com

abdopublishing.com

Published by Abdo Publishing, a division of ABDO, PO Box 398166, Minneapolis, Minnesota 55439. Copyright © 2017 by Abdo Consulting Group, Inc. International copyrights reserved in all countries. No part of this book may be reproduced in any form without written permission from the publisher. Core Library™ is a trademark and logo of Abdo Publishing.

Printed in the United States of America, North Mankato, Minnesota
032016
092016

Cover Photo: SuperStock/Glow Images
Interior Photos: SuperStock/Glow Images, 1; National Geographic Creative/Corbis, 4, 45; Arnold Lorne Hicks/GraphicaArtis/Corbis, 7; North Wind Picture Archives, 10, 17, 24, 28, 35; C. Schuessele Lith./Library of Congress, 13; Red Line Editorial, 18, 26; Ron Embleton (1930–88)/Private Collection/© Look and Learn/Bridgeman Images, 20; Corbis, 27; Universal History Archive/UIG/Bridgeman Images, 32; PVDE/Bridgeman Images, 37; AP Images, 38

Editor: Claire Mathiowetz
Series Designer: Ryan Gale

**Cataloging-in-Publication Data**
Names: Rea, Amy C., author.
Title: The Trail of Tears / by Amy C. Rea.
Description: Minneapolis, MN : Abdo Publishing, [2017] | Series: The wild West
     | Includes bibliographical references and index.
Identifiers: LCCN 2015960512 | ISBN 9781680782608 (lib. bdg.) |
     ISBN 9781680776713 (ebook)
Subjects:  LCSH:  Trail of Tears, 1838--Juvenile literature. | Cherokee Indians--
     Relocation--Juvenile literature. | Frontier and pioneer life ((U.S.)--Juvenile
     literature.
Classification: DDC 975.004/97557--dc23
LC record available at http://lccn.loc.gov/2015960512

# CONTENTS

# CHAPTER ONE

# THE CHEROKEE NATION

In the early 1800s, Native American people known as Cherokees lived in the southeast United States. But many European immigrants were arriving or had already arrived in America. They wanted land of their own. Between 1830 and 1839, the Cherokee people were forced to leave their homelands. The US government moved them west to Oklahoma. The journey was long and hard. Thousands of Cherokees

The Trail of Tears was a devastating and tragic time for the Cherokee people.

died on the trail. The Cherokees call the journey "Alannah-duna-Dlo-Hilu-I." In Cherokee this means "the trail where they cried."

## The Cherokees in the Southeast

The first written records of the Cherokees date to 1540. European settlers wrote about the native people of America. However, the Cherokee lived in these areas long before that.

The Cherokees survived on what they could find in nature. The men hunted and fished. They used every part of the animals. Deer provided meat for food. Deer also provided leather for blankets and clothing. People used animals bones or antlers to make

### Cherokee Farmers

Farming was an important part of the Cherokee lifestyle. The Cherokees likely began farming as early as 3000 BCE. Women who harvested wild plants learned how to take the seeds from plants and grow them. This made for more dependable crops. The farmers could keep seeds from year to year. They no longer had to search for wild plants.

Corn was very important to many Native Americans, as they ate it at almost every meal and even had religious ceremonies based on the vegetable.

tools. Sinews were used for thread to sew and weave. Some items, such as teeth and feathers, could not be used in practical ways. The Cherokees used them as decorations or in religious ceremonies.

The Cherokee women grew crops. These included corn, beans, and squash. They wove river canes, a bamboo-like plant, into baskets and mats.

# PERSPECTIVES

## The Importance of Nature

The Cherokees valued nature. They held six ceremonies each year to honor nature and give thanks. They also believed the four directions had meanings. South meant peace and happiness. East meant success. North stood for trouble and loss. And west represented death.

They shaped clay from rivers into pots. The women fired the pots in their fireplaces, much like potters today use kilns. They collected herbs to use as medicine.

## Cherokee Beliefs

Cherokee religious beliefs were rooted in nature. They believed that the Great Spirit created the land. They believed in many nature gods. The gods were in mountains, the sun, fire, and even individual plants.

The Cherokees believed it was important to use only what they needed. They did not want to take too much from nature. Each year they held several religious ceremonies. They celebrated growing seasons and other important events. One of the most significant was the Green Corn Ceremony. This celebrated the annual corn harvest.

## Life among Other Native Americans

Other tribes lived nearby. They included the Chickasaws, the Choctaws, the Creeks, and the Seminoles. These tribes did not always get along. Sometimes they fought wars over land. But none of these battles caused as much destruction as the arrival of Europeans.

## FURTHER EVIDENCE

Think about what you have read in this chapter. Native Americans have had their own land, traditions, and religion for thousands of years. There are many stories from Cherokee people on what they believe. Take a look at the website below. How does the information compare to what you read in this chapter?

**Cherokee Traditional Beliefs**
mycorelibrary.com/trail-of-tears

# CHAPTER TWO

# ARRIVAL OF THE EUROPEANS

Spanish explorer Hernando de Soto arrived in America in 1540. This was the first meeting between the Cherokees and Europeans. But centuries passed before the Cherokees had regular encounters with settlers. In the late 1600s, they began meeting and trading more with the Europeans. This led to unexpected problems. Diseases began

Hernando de Soto was believed to have met the Cherokees when he passed through their land in the state known today as Tennessee.

spreading in Cherokee communities. The most deadly was smallpox.

Explorers from Europe unknowingly brought smallpox. It was devastating to the Cherokees. They had never experienced the disease before. This meant their immune systems could not fight it. Approximately 7,000 to 10,000 Cherokees died from smallpox in the mid-1700s. That was nearly half of the Cherokee tribe.

The Cherokees did not know how to handle this terrible disease. The *didanawisgi*, or medicine men, could not cure it. This was even more frightening to them. But to the Europeans, the reduced number of Cherokee people meant more land would be free for settling.

## The Cherokees Side with the British

Smallpox was not the only problem. As more Europeans arrived, conflicts arose between them. The French and the British both claimed land in America.

Smallpox wiped out thousands of Native Americans in the 1700s.

Both sides wanted the Cherokees to side with them. For a while, the Cherokees fought for one side or the other. But in 1730, the Cherokees sent seven representatives to England to make a formal alliance. They agreed they would fight on behalf of the British.

## The Cherokees in Wars

The Cherokees supported the British in the French and Indian War (1754–1763). But during that war, the Cherokees faced anger from British colonists. The Cherokees and British accused each other of betrayal. This led to additional conflicts for the Cherokees. The Cherokees lost many lives fighting in the war. The British eventually defeated the French and took control of America.

However, the Cherokee loyalty to the British soon caused more problems. The war cost the British a great deal of money. To pay these debts, the British increased taxes on the colonies. The American colonists revolted against the British. This was the start of the American Revolutionary War (1775–1783). This war was disastrous for the Cherokees. They again fought for the British. They lost many tribe members. Entire villages were lost. When the British lost the war, the new nation of the United States controlled the east coast of America. The Cherokees negotiated peace settlements in 1791 with the United States. Another agreement was made in 1798. It cost them much of their land.

## Forced to Change

European immigrants continued arriving after the Revolutionary War. The Cherokees were repeatedly asked to give up land. US Secretary of War Henry Knox saw that this might lead to another war. He argued that the Cherokees needed to learn to live as the Europeans did.

The Europeans wanted the Cherokees to give up their culture. The Cherokees were told to wear European-style clothing. They had to learn

## PERSPECTIVES
### Revolutionary War

When the Revolutionary War started, members of the Cherokee tribe were divided. Many knew that the war would bring even more loss of land. Some wanted to stay out of the conflict completely. Others saw the war as a chance to prevent colonists from stealing more territory. They eventually sided with the British, who supported their need for land.

English, even though they had their own language. The Cherokees also had their own alphabet, which was invented by a Cherokee man named Sequoyah. The Cherokees had to give up their spiritual beliefs and convert to Christianity. Knox believed Native Americans were uncivilized. He thought they needed to change to become part of US society.

Some Cherokees were willing to make these changes. They had lost many of their people and homes in the wars. They thought learning new skills would let them live in peace. But this did

## Sequoyah and the Cherokee Language

Sequoyah was interested in how white people could write things on paper to communicate. He told other Cherokees that he could create symbols for sounds in the Cherokee language. They did not believe him. But he worked out more than 80 different symbols. Those symbols, like letters, could be combined to write words. This was called a syllabary. He wanted to use it to preserve Cherokee history and traditions.

Sequoyah was working as a silversmith when he invented the Cherokee alphabet.

not stop the Europeans from taking their land. The tensions continued.

## Gold Rush

In the 1820s, gold was discovered on Cherokee land in Georgia. Prospectors swarmed the area. Georgia governor George Gilmer eventually banned both whites and Native Americans from digging for gold.

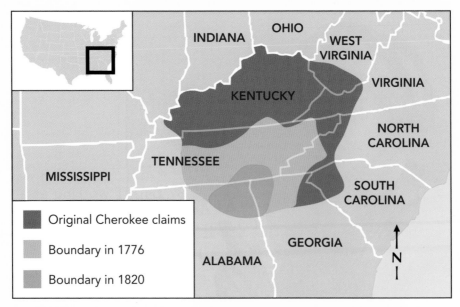

**Loss of Land**

As more and more Europeans arrived, the demand for land took a toll on the Cherokees. Look at this map to see how much of their land was taken away before they were forced to move west.

Georgia's state government took control of the areas with gold.

The US government had signed treaties that gave the Cherokees rights to their traditional land. But the gold rush caused states to ignore these treaties. Even states without gold did not want the Cherokees to live there. White settlers wanted access to all the land in the region, whether or not gold was involved. But the Cherokees wanted to keep the land that had been promised to them. The Cherokees, led by Principal Chief John Ross, filed lawsuits to keep their land. These lawsuits went to the US Supreme Court. But the US government began looking for ways to remove the Cherokees from the southeast United States. It planned to send them northwest.

## EXPLORE ONLINE

To the British, part of the value of having the Cherokees as an ally was in their strength and stamina. Cherokee warriors could run long distances and cover a lot of ground. The Cherokee could deliver messages, scout locations, and monitor enemy movement. In return, the British provided various goods, such as brass kettles, hoes, scissors, and knives. Take a look at the Cherokee role in the French and Indian War at the following website. What new information did you learn about the Cherokee relationship with the British?

**The Cherokees and the French and Indian War**
mycorelibrary.com/trail-of-tears

# CHAPTER THREE

# THE TRAIL
# OF TEARS

The process of removing the Cherokees began in 1830 when the US Congress passed the Indian Removal Act. President Andrew Jackson strongly supported this act. It gave him the ability to negotiate with the tribes in the southeast. He wanted to force them to move west. The act provided $500,000 to establish new territories in the West and pay Native American landowners for what they would lose.

Many Native Americans had to endure harsh weather on their journeys.

## The Old Settlers

Most of the Cherokees did not want to leave. They had lived on their land for centuries. They had built homes, farms, and businesses. When the Cherokees were told to learn European ways, many had done so. They felt this would protect them.

However, some Cherokees left the southeast voluntarily. The US government offered money and supplies to those who left freely. In 1834 the first group of Cherokees prepared to move to the Indian Territory in what is now Oklahoma. These early groups became known as the Old Settlers. They faced many hardships, including an outbreak of measles. As with smallpox, the Cherokees had not been exposed to measles before.

Other groups met similar problems. A group that set out in October 1837 faced not only disease, but also rain and snow. Some who left for the West turned around and came home. The stories they told made other Cherokees fearful of leaving.

## Forced Removal Begins

Thousands of Cherokees remained in the southeast. They waited as lawsuits went to the Supreme Court. They hoped they would be allowed to stay. The Treaty of New Echota was a treaty signed with the US government in 1835. It gave the Cherokees two years to leave. This treaty was signed by a small group of Cherokees. Most of the Cherokees did not agree with the treaty. They were angry with those who had signed it. By 1838 very

## PERSPECTIVES
### The Treaty of New Echota Resistance

In 1836 Cherokee Principal Chief John Ross wrote a letter to the US House of Representatives. He described his strong disapproval of the Treaty of New Echota. A small number of Cherokees had signed a treaty most disagreed with. In his letter he wrote,

> We are stripped of every attribute of freedom and eligibility for legal self-defense. Our property may be plundered before our eyes; violence may be committed on our persons; even our lives may be taken away, and there is none to regard our complaints.

John Ross became Principal Chief of the Cherokee Nation in 1828.

few Cherokees had left. The government decided to act.

President Martin Van Buren ordered the army to begin removing tribes. Soldiers forcibly removed the Cherokees from their homes. The soldiers put the Cherokees in stockades to await the move west. The Native Americans were taken from their homes, businesses, and farms. They were not allowed to take any private belongings. They could not say good-bye to anyone. If some family members were away, including children, the remaining family members were taken without waiting. In some cases, soldiers brought bedding and clothing for the Native Americans. In other cases, nothing was allowed.

Conditions in the stockades were terrible. People were crowded very close together. They had no privacy. They had to remain outdoors despite harsh weather. They were then moved from stockades to internment camps. There they were held for days or weeks before moving west. People suffered from many diseases, including dysentery, whooping cough, and measles. Many died.

## A Horrible Journey

The Cherokees had been promised land in the Indian Territory. It was nearly 1,000 miles (1,609 km) from their homeland. There were several routes to the territory. Some were by river, and some were by land. But none were easy.

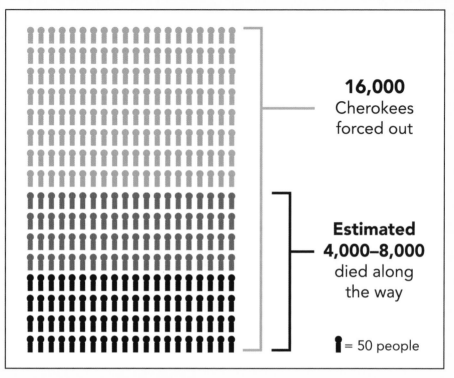

**16,000** Cherokees forced out

**Estimated 4,000–8,000** died along the way

= 50 people

**Death by the Thousands**
The Cherokees were forced out of their homes by the thousands. Take a look at the numbers above. What percent of Cherokees died along the way?

The journey by boat was interrupted by low water in the Arkansas River. Travelers had to unload and continue by land. Cholera, a disease that results from unclean water, killed more than 50 people.

Low rivers were not the only risk on the water routes. The boats were also severely overcrowded. Their wooden structures would begin to crack under

When Native Americans did not have boats, they had to cross rivers by walking and swimming across, even with horses.

the strain. Traveling during intense summer heat and droughts was even more difficult. Illness continued to cause deaths.

Those traveling by land faced a different set of dangers. Some felt traveling by land in the heat of the summer was not a good idea. So the Cherokees waited until fall. They also felt that there would be more animals to hunt in the autumn. This would feed people along the way. The Cherokees remained in the

Native Americans traveled in large groups when they were forced out of their homes.

camps until late September. However, since they had not been allowed to bring their belongings, many of them did not have warm clothing. They also lacked winter shoes, cooking supplies, and tents.

Things became even worse when it rained. The dirt roads on which people traveled became muddy. It was difficult to get horses and wagons through the mud. There was not enough food for people or their animals. Whites along the route took advantage of the Cherokees. They demanded money or took their horses.

A drought in the summer caused water to be scarce. Sometimes the water was dirty and made people sick. Even healthy people became ill after walking for miles in the cold, wet weather. A few doctors traveled with the Cherokees. But there were not nearly enough of them to cope with all the sick people.

People died frequently. There was little time to bury the dead. Entire families were wiped out. Other

## Other Tribes

The Cherokees were not the only people to face terrible losses. Many of the other tribes who were forcibly removed from the southeastern United States also suffered death and hardship. Of the 3,000 Chickasaws who left for Oklahoma, 500 died of dysentery and smallpox. The Choctaws lost 2,000 tribe members. The Creeks lost 3,500. Altogether, tens of thousands of Native Americans died because of resettling.

families had to leave the bodies of loved ones behind. Some historians believe approximately 4,000 Cherokees died during the move. This number came from a missionary, Dr. Elizur Butler, who accompanied them. Other historians believe the number could be as high as 10,000.

Arrival in the Indian Territory did not bring joy or relief. Between the hardship of the journey and all they had lost, the Cherokees were exhausted and mournful. And their lives were not about to improve.

Josephine Lattimer, a member of the Choctaw nation, gave an interview about the removal on October 13, 1937:

> *In loading my people got separated from each other for there were hundreds of wagons on this journey. When they reached the Ouachita . . . River, it was on a rampage and out of banks. The roads were almost impassable. It was raining and cold. Even for all the well and strong, the journey was almost beyond human endurance. Many were weak and broken-hearted, and as night came there were new [graves] dug beside the way. Many of the Indians contracted pneumonia fever and the cholera.*

Source: Lorrie Montiero. *"Family Stories from the Trail of Tears."* American Native Press Archives and Sequoyah National Research Center. *University of Arkansas at Little Rock, n.d. Web. Accessed February 17, 2016.*

## Consider Your Audience

Review this passage closely. Consider how you would adapt it for a different audience, such as your parents, your principal, or younger friends. Write a blog post conveying this same information for the new audience. What is the most effective way to get your point across to this audience? How does your new approach differ from the original text and why?

# CHAPTER FOUR

# LIFE AFTER RESETTLEMENT

The Cherokees had been promised food rations from the government upon arrival. Rations were provided, but there were many problems. Food was only delivered every other month. Sometimes it arrived weeks behind schedule. This created problems for those who did not have a way to store the food. Dishonest contractors sometimes kept part of the rations for themselves.

Examples of the dwellings Native Americans lived in when they reached the Indian Territory

### "Cherokee Golden Age"

In the years after the Trail of Tears, the Cherokees entered into what some call the "Cherokee Golden Age." It was a time of prosperity for the Cherokees, where they rebuilt their lives. Their economic, political, and educational systems developed greatly. This lasted until the US Civil War (1861–1865), when even more land was taken from the Cherokees. However, other Cherokees disagree that this was a time of success and good fortune. Instead, they believe that this was a time when the Cherokees lost their traditional way of life. They believe that the true golden age of the Cherokees was before the Europeans came to North America.

The Cherokees knew the plants and animals of the southeastern United States very well. But they did not know this new territory. They did not know how to find safe plants to eat or game to hunt. Those arriving in the fall were too late to plant crops.

## Problems within the New Cherokee Nation

Months passed, and the Cherokees still faced many challenges. They found that farming the new Cherokee Nation was very different from

Despite the many setbacks the Indian Territory caused, the land did provide new animals for Native Americans to hunt, such as the buffalo.

farming in their old home. Floods frequently washed away crops planted near rivers. The Cherokees lacked the farm tools they needed, such as heavy plows. The horses and oxen they brought were starving and ill.

There were also bad feelings between the Old Settlers and those who had been forced to leave. The Cherokees who had wanted to stay in the southeast felt that the Old Settlers had betrayed them. They felt that all Cherokees should have stayed and fought for the rights to their land.

The Old Settlers had also benefited from being compensated by the government for their willingness to leave. They arrived in New Cherokee Nation with some money and tools to build new farms. Those forced to leave arrived with almost nothing.

## Cherokee Tension

Much resentment had grown between the Old Settlers and the Cherokees who arrived later. The onset of the Civil War brought about even more anger. Some of the Cherokee fought for the Confederacy. Others did not.

In 1887 Congress passed the Dawes Act. This act allowed President Grover Cleveland to divide Native American lands into allotments. Then individual members of Native American tribes would own land. Often these allotments were much smaller than what the Native Americans had originally. Individual Native

A few Cherokee men going to meet with the US government to sign a treaty in 1866

Wilma Mankiller served as deputy chief of the Cherokee Nation from 1983 to 1985.

Americans who accepted an allotment were granted US citizenship. The president's intention was to have Native Americans become part of the US population. But it undermined tribal government and policies. It also reduced the amount of land owned by tribes. More and more white people were given land once owned by Native Americans.

## Modern-Day Cherokees

In 1907 Oklahoma became the 46th state. The government

## Wilma Mankiller

In spite of all that was done to the Cherokees, they have survived. They have also honored their roots and traditions. Women have always been important to Cherokee culture. In 1985 Wilma Mankiller was named the first female principal chief. She was a popular leader who worked hard to improve Cherokee health, government, and education. Women's rights were also very important to her. She was reelected twice. In 1995 she stepped down due to poor health. However, she continued to be an advocate for the Cherokee. She taught at Dartmouth University and wrote books until her death in 2010.

continued to allot small parcels of land to Native Americans. However, many parcels were given to people who did not have strong proof of Cherokee ancestry. By the 1970s, the Cherokees had lost more than 19 million acres (7,689,027 ha) of land. The part of Oklahoma that was supposed to belong only to the Cherokees did not exist anymore.

Yet the Cherokees themselves survived. Today there are more than 300,000 Cherokees in the world. Approximately 70,000 still live in Oklahoma. The Trail of Tears is a devastating part of their past—one that will never be forgotten.

In an interview in 1937, Elizabeth Watts recalls the story her grandparents told her about their experience on the Trail of Tears:

> The road they traveled, History calls the "Trail of Tears."
> This trail was more than tears. It was death, sorrow, hunger,
> exposure, and humiliation to a civilized people as were
> the Cherokees. Today, our greatest politicians, lawyers,
> doctors, and many of worthy mention are Cherokees.
> Holding high places, in spite of all the humiliation brought
> on their forefathers. . . . Lands promised, money promised,
> never materialized only with a paltry sum, too small
> to recall, for what they parted with and the treatment
> received.

Source: Lorrie Montiero. "Family Stories from the Trail of Tears." American Native Press Archives and Sequoyah National Research Center. *University of Arkansas at Little Rock, n.d. Web. Accessed February 17, 2016.*

## Back It Up

The author of this passage is using evidence to support a point. Write a paragraph describing the point the author is making. Then write down two or three pieces of evidence the author uses to make the point.

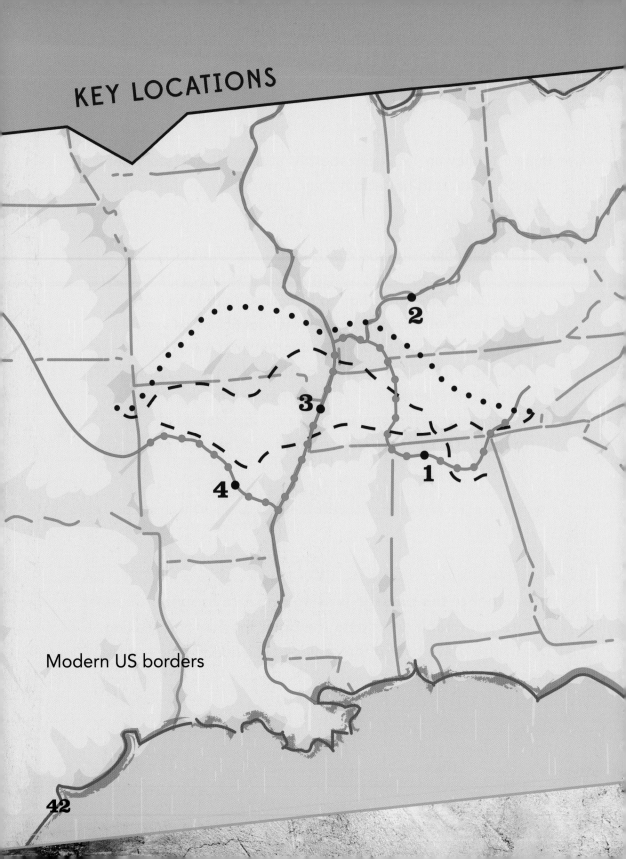

Modern US borders

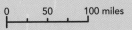

N

0    50    100 miles

The Trail of Tears

● ● ●  Land route

●─●─●  Water route

─ ─ ─  Other major routes

1.    Tennessee River

2.    Ohio River

3.    Mississippi River

4.    Arkansas River

# STOP AND THINK

## Tell the Tale

Chapter Three talks about the Cherokees being taken from their homes and sent to stockades. Write 200 words about this as if it happened to you. How would you feel? What would you do?

## Surprise Me

Chapter One talks about different aspects of the Cherokee life, including their religious beliefs. After reading this chapter, what two or three ideas did you find most surprising? Write a few sentences about each idea. Why did you find each one surprising?

## Dig Deeper

After reading this book, what questions do you still have about the Trail of Tears? With an adult's help, find a few reliable sources that can help answer your questions. Write a paragraph about what you learned.

## Say What?

Studying the Cherokees and the Trail of Tears can mean learning a lot of new vocabulary words. Find five words in this book you had never heard before. Use a dictionary to find out what they mean. Then write the meanings in your own words and use each word in a new sentence.

# GLOSSARY

**alliance**
when two or more groups
of people join together for a
common cause

**colonists**
people who settle in one
country that is either owned
or controlled by another
country far away

**drought**
an extended period of time
without rain

**internment camp**
a large camp meant to hold
many people without a trial
during a war

**prospectors**
people who search an area
for natural resources, such as
gold

**rations**
specified amounts of things,
like food, determined by the
government and given out in
regular portions

**sinew**
tough fiber in the body that
connects muscles or bones

**stockades**
enclosures or pens where
prisoners are kept

**treaty**
an agreement made by
negotiation

**tribes**
groups of people who have
the same language, customs,
and beliefs; often composed
of family members

# LEARN MORE

## Books

Johnston, Carolyn Ross. *Voices of Cherokee Women.* Winston-Salem, NC: John F. Blair Publisher, 2013.

Tieck, Sarah. *Cherokee.* North Mankato, MN: Abdo Publishing, 2014.

Vander Hook, Sue. *Trail of Tears.* North Mankato, MN: Abdo Publishing, 2010.

## Websites

To learn more about the Wild West, visit **booklinks.abdopublishing.com**. These links are routinely monitored and updated to provide the most current information available.

Visit **mycorelibrary.com** for free additional tools for teachers and students.

# INDEX

# ABOUT THE AUTHOR

Amy C. Rea grew up in northern Minnesota and now lives in a Minneapolis suburb with her husband, two sons, and dog. She has written about the lost colonists of Roanoke and the lost continent of Atlantis.